Tho' nine in ten, are oft'ner found to kill.—
Yet Puff's the word, which gives at least a name,
And oftener gains the undeserving Fame:
Or wherefore read we of Lord Fanny's Taste,
Of me—an Actor—wonderfully chaste!
And yet so squeamish is our Lady elf,
She'd rather die—than paragraph herself;
So fix'd on me—the Prologue speaking Hack,
To stop, with Puff direct, the Critic Pack,
Who yelp, and foaming, bark from morn to night,
And when run hard—turn tail—then snap and bite;
Putting the timid Hare-like-Bard to flight.
To such, the best and only Puff to hit,
Is that which honest CANDOUR must admit,
A Female Scribbler is an harmless Wit;
And who so harmless as our present Bard,
Claiming no greater or distinct reward,
Than what from free Translation is her due,
Which here in fullest trust she leaves to you:
With this remark—Who own their Debts with pride,
Are well entitled to the Credit Side.
And as for those with whom she makes so free
They'll ne'er complain of English Liberty;
But glory to behold their Tinsel shine,
Through the rich Bullion of the English Line.
Fear then avaunt! Trust to a BRITISH JURY—
With them, an honest Verdict I'll ensure you:
Let Echo catch the sound—'Tis PRATT enacts,
You're Judges of the Law, as well as Facts.
On this she rests her Cause, and hopes to find,
As Friends, and Next Door Neighbours, you'll be kind;
At least, this only punishment-ensure,
A Frown—and that's severe enough, from you.
Thus puff'd—I freely to the Court commit her,
Not doubting, as a Woman, you'll acquit her—
And now join issue, Sirs, without delay—
Judging from written Evidence our Play,
And—send her a good Diliverance, I pray.

ACT I

SCENE I - An Anti-Chamber at Sir George Splendorville's, Adjoining a Ball-Room

Enter **BLUNTLY**, meeting a **SERVANT** in Livery.

BLUNTLY

Come, come, is not every thing ready? Is not the ball-room prepared yet? It is past ten o'clock.

SERVANT
We have only to fix up the new chandelier.

BLUNTLY
I'll have no new chandelier.

SERVANT
My master said the last ball he gave, the company were in the dark.

BLUNTLY
And if you blind them with too much light, they will be in the dark still.

SERVANT
The musicians, sir, wish for some wine.

BLUNTLY
What, before the ball begins? No, tell them if they are tipsy at the end of it, it will be quite soon enough.

SERVANT
You are always so cross, Mr. Bluntly, when my master is going to have company.

BLUNTLY
Have not I a right to be cross? For while the whole house is in good humour, if there was not one person cross enough to take a little care, every thing would be wasted and ruined through extreme good temper.

[A **MAN** crosses the stage.

Here, you—Mister—Pray are you the person who was sent with the chandelier?

SHOPMAN
Yes, sir.

BLUNTLY
Then please to take it back again—We don't want it.

SHOPMAN
What is your objection to it, sir?

BLUNTLY
It will cost too much.

SHOPMAN
Mr. Bluntly, all the trades-people are more frightened at you than at your master.—Sir George, Heaven bless him! never cares how much a thing costs.

BLUNTLY
That is, because he never cares whether he pays for it or not—but if he did, depend upon it he would be very particular. Tradesmen all wish to be paid for their ware, don't they?

SHOPMAN
Certainly, sir.

BLUNTLY
Then why will they force so many unnecessary things, and make so many extravagant charges as to put all power of payment out of the question?

[Enter **EVANS**. The **TRADESMAN** goes off at the opposite Door.

BLUNTLY [Sullenly]
How do you do, Mrs. Evans?

EVANS
What makes you sigh, Mr. Bluntly?

BLUNTLY
What makes you smile?

EVANS
To see all the grand preparations for the ball this evening. I anticipate the joy my lady will take here, and I smile for her.

BLUNTLY
And I sigh for my master.—I foresee all the bills that will be brought in, for this evening's expence, and I anticipate the sorrow it will one day be to him.

EVANS
But consider, Mr. Bluntly, your master has my lady's fortune to take.

BLUNTLY
Yes, but I consider he has your lady to take along with it; and I prophecy one will stick by him some time after the other is gone.

EVANS
For shame.—My lady, I have no doubt, will soon cure Sir George of his extravagance.

BLUNTLY
It will then be by taking away the means.—Why, Lady Caroline is as extravagant as himself.

EVANS
You are mistaken.—She never gives routs, masquerades, balls, or entertainments of any kind.

BLUNTLY
But she constantly goes to them whenever she is invited.

EVANS

That, I call but a slight imprudence.—She has no wasteful indiscretions like Sir George. For instance, she never makes a lavish present.

BLUNTLY

No, but she takes a lavish present, as readily as if she did.

EVANS

And surely you cannot call that imprudence?

BLUNTLY

No, I call it something worse.

EVANS

Then, although she loves gaming to distraction, and plays deep, yet she never loses.

BLUNTLY

No, but she always wins—and that I call something worse.

[A loud rapping at the street-door.

EVANS

Here's the company. Will you permit me, Mr. Bluntly, to stand in one corner, and have a peep at them?

BLUNTLY

If you please.

[Rapping again.

What spirit there is in that, Rat, tat, tat, tat.—And what life, frolic, and joy, the whole house is going to experience except myself. As for me, I am ready to cry at the thoughts of it all.

[Exit.

[Enter **LADY CAROLINE**.

LADY CAROLINE

Here, the first of the company. I am sorry for it.

[**EVANS** comes forward.

Evans, what has brought you hither?

EVANS

I came, my lady, to see the preparations making on your account—for it is upon your account alone, that Sir George gives this grand fête.

LADY CAROLINE

Why, I do flatter myself it is.—But where is he? What is it o'clock?—It was impossible to stay at the stupid opera.—How do I look? I once did intend to wear those set of diamonds Sir George presented me with the other morning—but then, I reflected again, that if—

EVANS

Ah, my lady, what a charming thing to have such a lover—Sir George prevents every wish—he must make the best of husbands.

LADY CAROLINE

And yet my father wishes to break off the marriage—he talks of his prodigality—and, certainly, Sir George lives above his income.

EVANS

But then, Madam, so does every body else.

LADY CAROLINE

But Sir George ought undoubtedly to change his conduct, and not be thus continually giving balls and entertainments—and inviting to his table acquaintance, that not only come to devour his dinners and suppers, but him.

EVANS

And there are people malicious enough to call your ladyship one of his devourers too.

LADY CAROLINE

As a treaty of marriage is so nearly concluded between us, I think, Mrs. Evans, I am at liberty to visit Sir George, or to receive his presents, without having my character, or my delicacy called in question.

[A loud rapping.

The company are coming: is it not strange he is not here to receive them.

[Exit **EVANS**.

[Enter **TWO LADIES** and a **GENTLEMAN**, who curtsy and bow to **LADY CAROLINE**.—**SIR GEORGE** enters at the opposite door, magnificently dressed.

SIR GEORGE

Ladies, I entreat your pardon; dear Lady Caroline excuse me. I have been in the country all the morning, and have had scarce time to return to town and dress for your reception.

[Another rapping.

[Enter **MR. LUCRE**, **LORD HAZARD**, **LADY BRIDGET SQUANDER**, &C.

SIR GEORGE

Dear Lucre, I am glad to see you.

MR. LUCRE
My dear Sir George, I had above ten engagements this evening, but they all gave place to your invitation.

SIR GEORGE
Thank you.—My dear Lady Bridget—

LADY BRIDGET
It is impossible to resist an invitation from the most polished man alive.

[**SIR GEORGE** bows.

What a superb dress! (in his hearing, as he turns away) and what an elegant deportment.

MR. LUCRE [After speaking apart with **SIR GEORGE**]
No, I am not in a state to take any part at Pharo—I am ruin'd.—Would you believe it Sir George, I am not worth a farthing in the world.

SIR GEORGE
Yes, I believed it long ago.

MR. LUCRE
Now we are on that subject—could you lend me a hundred pounds?

SIR GEORGE [Taking out his pocket-book]
I have about me, only this bill for two hundred.

MR. LUCRE
That will do as well—I am not circumstantial.

[Takes it.

And my dear Sir George command my purse at any time—all it contains, will ever be at your service.

SIR GEORGE
I thank you.

MR. LUCRE
Nay, though I have no money of my own, yet you know I can always raise friends—and by heaven! my dear Sir George, I often wish to see you reduced to my circumstances, merely to prove how much I could, and would, do to serve you.

SIR GEORGE
I sincerely thank you.

MR. LUCRE
And one can better ask a favour for one's friend than for one's-self, you know: for when one wants to borrow money on one's own account, there are so many little delicacies to get the better of—such as I

felt just now.—I was as pale as death, I dare say, when I asked you for this money—did not you perceive I was?

SIR GEORGE
I can't say I did.

MR. LUCRE
But you must have observed I hesitated, and looked very foolish.

SIR GEORGE
I thought for my part, that I looked as foolish.—But I hope I did not hesitate.

MR. LUCRE
Nor ever will, when a friend applys to you, I'll answer for it—Nor ever shall a friend hesitate when you apply.

LORD HAZARD [Taking **SIR GEORGE** aside]
The obligations I am under to you for extricating me from that dangerous business—

SIR GEORGE
Never name it.

LORD HAZARD
Not only name it, Sir George, but shortly I hope to return the kindness; and, if I do but live—

SIR GEORGE [To the **COMPANY**]
Permit me to conduct you to the next apartment.

LADY CAROLINE
Most willingly, Sir George. I was the first who arrived; which proves my eagerness to dance.

SIR GEORGE [Aside to her]
But let me hope, passion for dancing was not the only one, that caused your impatience.

[As the **COMPANY** move towards the ball-room, **Mr. LUCRE** and **LORD HAZARD** come forward.

MR. LUCRE
Oh! there never was such a man in the world as the master of this house; there never was such a friendly, generous, noble heart; he has the best heart in the world, and the best taste in dress.

[The **COMPANY** Exeunt, and the music is heard to begin.

SCENE II - An Apartment, Which Denotes the Poverty of the Inhabitants

HENRY and **ELEANOR** discovered.

ELEANOR
It is very late and very cold too, brother; and yet we have neither of us heart to bid each other good night.

HENRY
No—beds were made for rest.

ELEANOR
And that noise of carriages and link-boys at Sir George Splendorville's, next door, would keep us awake, if our sorrows did not.

HENRY
The poor have still more to complain of, when chance throws them thus near the rich,—it forces upon their minds a comparison might drive them to despair, if—

ELEANOR
—If they should not have good sense enough to reflect, that all this bustle and show of pleasure, may fall very short of happiness; as all the distress we feel, has not yet, thank Heaven, reached to misery.

HENRY
What do you call it then?

ELEANOR
A trial; sent to make us patient.

HENRY
It may make you so, but cannot me. Good morning to you.

[Going.

ELEANOR
Nay, it is night yet. Where are you going?

HENRY
I don't know.—To take a walk.—The streets are not more uncomfortable than this place, and scarcely colder.

ELEANOR
Oh, my dear brother! I cannot express half the uneasiness I feel when you part from me, though but for the shortest space.

HENRY
Why?

ELEANOR
Because I know your temper; you are impatient under adversity; you rashly think providence is unkind; and you would snatch those favours, which are only valuable when bestowed.

HENRY
What do you mean?

ELEANOR
Nay, do not be angry; but every time you go out into this tempting town, where superfluous riches continually meet the eye of the poor, I tremble lest you should forfeit your honesty for that, which Heaven decreed should not belong to you.

HENRY
And if I did, you would despise and desert me?

ELEANOR
No: not desert you; for I am convinced you would only take, to bring to me; but this is to assure you, I do not want for any thing.

HENRY
Not want?—Nor does my father?

ELEANOR
Scarcely, while we visit him. Every time he sees us we make him happy; but he would never behold us again if we behaved unworthy of him.

HENRY
What! banish us from a prison?

ELEANOR
And although it is a prison, you could not be happy under such a restriction.

HENRY
Happy!—When was I happy last?

ELEANOR
Yesterday, when your father thanked you for your kindness to him. Did we not all three weep with affection for each other? and was not that happiness?

HENRY
It was—nor will I give up such satisfaction, for any enticement that can offer.—Be contented, Eleanor,—for your sake and my father's, I will be honest.—Nay, more,—I will be scrupulously proud—and that line of conduct which my own honour could not force me to follow, my love to you and him, shall compel me to.—When, through necessity, I am tempted to plunder, your blushes and my father's anguish shall hold my hand.—And when I am urged through impatience, to take away my own life, your lingering death and his, shall check the horrid suggestion, and I will live for you.

ELEANOR
Then do not ever trust yourself away, at least from one of us.

HENRY

Dear sister! do you imagine that your power is less when separated from me? Do you suppose I think less frequently on my father and his dismal prison, because we are not always together? Oh! no! he comes even more forcibly to my thoughts in his absence—and then, more bitterly do I feel his misery, than while the patient old man, before my eyes, talks to me of his consolations; his internal comforts from a conscience pure, a mind without malice, and a heart, where every virtue occupy a place.—Therefore, do not fear that I shall forget either him or you, though I might possibly forget myself.

[Exit.

ELEANOR
If before him I am cheerful, yet to myself I must complain.

[Weeps.

And that sound of festivity at the house adjoining is insupportable! especially when I reflect that a very small portion of what will be wasted there only this one night, would be sufficient to give my dear father liberty.

[A rapping at the door of her chamber, on the opposite entrance.

ELEANOR
Who's there?

MR. BLACKMAN [Without]
Open the door.

ELEANOR
The voice of our landlord.

[Goes to the door.

Is it you, Mr. Blackman?

BLACKMAN
Yes, open the door.

[Rapping louder.

[She opens it: **BLACKMAN** enters, followed by **BLUNTLY**.

BLACKMAN
What a time have you made me wait!—And in the name of wonder, why do you lock your door? Have you any thing to lose? Have not you already sold all the furniture you brought hither? And are you afraid of being stolen yourself?

[**ELEANOR** retires to the back of the Stage.

BLUNTLY

Is this the chamber?

BLACKMAN
Yes, Sir, yes, Mr. Bluntly, this is it.

[**BLACKMAN** assumes a very different tone of voice in speaking to **BLUNTLY** and **ELEANOR**; to the one he is all submissive humility, to the other all harshness.

BLUNTLY [Contemptuously]
This!

BLACKMAN
Why yes, sir,—this is the only place I have left in my own house, since your master has been pleased to occupy that next door, while his own magnificent one has been repairing.—Lock yourself up, indeed!

[Looking at **ELEANOR**.

—You have been continually asking me for more rooms, Mr. Bluntly, and have not I made near half a dozen doors already from one house to the other, on purpose to accommodate your good family.— Upon my honour, I have not now a single chamber but what I have let to these lodgers, and what I have absolute occasion for myself.

BLUNTLY
And if you do put yourself to a little inconvenience, Mr. Blackman, surely my master—

BLACKMAN
Your master, Mr. Bluntly, is a very good man—a very generous man—and I hope at least he has found me a very lucky one; for good luck is all the recommendation which I, in my humble station, aspire to— and since I have been Sir George's attorney, I have gained him no less than two law-suits.

BLUNTLY
I know it. I know also that you have lost him four.

BLACKMAN
We'll drop the subject.—And in regard to this room, sir, it does not suit, you say?

BLUNTLY
No, for I feel the cold wind blow through every crevice.

BLACKMAN
But suppose I was to have it put a little into repair? That window, for instance, shall have a pane or two of glass put in; the cracks of the door shall be stopt up; and then every thing will have a very different appearance.

BLUNTLY
And why has not this been done before?

BLACKMAN

Would you have me be laying out my money, while I only let the place at a paltry price, to people who I am obliged to threaten to turn into the streets every quarter, before I can get my rent from them?

BLUNTLY
Is that the situation of your lodgers at present?

BLACKMAN
Yes.—But they made a better appearance when they first came, or I had not taken such persons to live thus near to your master.

BLUNTLY
That girl—
[Looking at **ELEANOR**]
—seems very pretty—and I dare say my master would not care if he was nearer to her.

BLACKMAN
Pshaw, pshaw—she is a poor creature—she is in great distress. She is misery itself.

BLUNTLY
I feel quite charmed with misery.—Who belongs to her?

BLACKMAN
A young man who says he is her brother—very likely he is not—but that I should not enquire about, if they could pay my rent. If people will pay me, I don't care what they are.
[Addressing himself to **ELEANOR**]
I desire you will tell your brother when he comes in, that I have occasion for the money which will be due to me to-morrow—and if I don't receive it before to-morrow night, he must seek some other habitation.

BLUNTLY
Hush, Mr. Blackman—if you speak so loud, you will have our company in the next house hear you.

BLACKMAN
And if they did, do you think it would spoil their dancing? No, Mr. Bluntly.—And in that respect, I am a person of fashion.—I never suffer any distress to interfere with my enjoyments.

ELEANOR [Coming to him]
Dear sir, have but patience a little while longer.—Indeed, I hope you will lose nothing.

BLACKMAN
I won't lose any thing.

[Going.

ELEANOR [Following him]
Sir, I would speak a single word to you, if you will be so good as to hear me?

BLUNTLY

Ay, stay and hear her.

ELEANOR [Looking at **BLUNTLY**]
But I wish to speak to him by ourselves.

BLUNTLY
Then I'll withdraw.

BLACKMAN [In anger]
What have you to say?

BLUNTLY
Hear her, Mr. Blackman—or may none of her sex ever listen to you.

[Exit.

BLACKMAN
If it is only to entreat me to let you continue here, I am gone in an instant.—Come, speak quickly, for I have no time to lose.—Come, speak, speak.

ELEANOR [Weeping]
But are you resolved to have no pity? You know in what a helpless situation we are—and the deplorable state of my poor father.

BLACKMAN
Ay, I thought what you had to say—farewel, farewel.

ELEANOR [Laying hold of him]
Oh! do not plunge us into more distress than we can bear; but open your heart to compassion.

BLACKMAN
I can't—'tis a thing I never did in my life.

[Going, he meets **BLUNTLY**, who stops him.

BLUNTLY
Well, have you granted her request?

BLACKMAN
I would do a great deal to oblige you, Mr. Bluntly—and if you will only give your word for the trifle of rent owing, why, I am not so hard-hearted but I will suffer her to stay.

BLUNTLY
Well, well,—I will give my word.

BLACKMAN
But remember, it is not to be put down to your master's account, but to your own.—I am not to give credit.

ELEANOR
Nor am I to lay my brother under an obligation of this nature.
[To **BLUNTLY**]
I thank you for your offer, sir, but I cannot accept it.

BLACKMAN [In extreme anger]
What do you mean by that?

BLUNTLY
Perhaps she is right.

ELEANOR
My brother would resent my acceptance of a favour from a stranger.

BLACKMAN
Your brother resent! A poor man resent! Did you ever hear of any body's regarding a poor man's resentment?

ELEANOR
No—nor a poor woman's prayers.

BLACKMAN
Yes, I will regard your prayers, if you will suffer this gentleman to be your friend.

ELEANOR
Any acquaintance of your's, Mr. Blackman, I must distrust.

BLACKMAN
Do you hear with what contempt she treats us both?

BLUNTLY
But perhaps she is right—at least, in treating one of us so, I am sure she is—and I will forgive her wronging the one, for the sake of her doing justice to the other.

[Enter **HENRY**: he starts at seeing **BLACKMAN** and **BLUNTLY**.

HENRY
Who are these?

BLACKMAN
"Who are these?" Did you ever hear such impertinence?

[Going up to him.

Pray who are you, sir?

HENRY

I am a man.

BLACKMAN
Yes—but I am a lawyer.

HENRY
Whatever you are, this apartment is mine, not your's—and I desire you to leave it.

BLACKMAN
But to-morrow it will be mine, and then I shall desire you to leave it, and force you to leave it.

HENRY
Eleanor, retire to the other chamber; I am sorry I left you.

[Leads her off.

BLACKMAN
And I am sorry that I and my friend should come here to be affronted.

BLUNTLY
Mr. Blackman, I won't be called names.

BLACKMAN
Names, sir! What names did I call you?

BLUNTLY
Did not you call me your friend? I assure you, sir, I am not used to be called names. I am but a servant whose character is every thing—and I'll let you know that I am not your friend.

BLACKMAN
Why, you blockhead, does not your master call himself my friend?

BLUNTLY
Yes, my master is a great man, and he can get a place without a character,—but if I lose mine, I am ruined; therefore take care how you miscal me for the future, for I assure you I won't bear it. I am not your friend, and you shall find I am not.

[Exit in great anger, **BLACKMAN** following.

ACT II

SCENE I - An Apartment at Sir George Splendorville's

Enter **SIR GEORGE**, followed by **BLUNTLY**.

SIR GEORGE [Rubbing his eyes]

What's o'clock?

BLUNTLY
Just noon, sir.

SIR GEORGE
Why was I waked so early?

BLUNTLY
You were not waked, sir—You rung.

SIR GEORGE
Then it was in my sleep—and could not you suppose so?—After going to bed at five, to make me rise at noon!
[In a violent passion]
What am I to do with myself, sir, till it is time to go out for the evening?

BLUNTLY
You have company to dinner you know, sir.

SIR GEORGE
No, it is to supper—and what am I to do with myself till that time?

BLUNTLY
Company again to supper, Sir?

SIR GEORGE
Yes, and the self-same company I had last night—I invited them upon Lady Caroline's account—to give her an opportunity of revenge, for the money she lost here yesterday evening—and I am all weariness—I am all lassitude and fretfulness till the time arrives.—But now I call to mind, I have an affair that may engage my attention a few hours. You were giving me an account, Bluntly, of that beautiful girl I saw enter at Blackman's?

BLUNTLY
Yes, sir, I saw her late last night in Mr. Blackman's house—she lodges there.

SIR GEORGE
Indeed? In Blackman's house? I am glad to hear it.

BLUNTLY
And he has assured me, sir, that she and her family are in the greatest poverty imaginable.

SIR GEORGE
I am glad to hear it.

BLUNTLY

They have been it seems above a twelvemonth in London, in search of some rich relations; but instead of meeting with them, the father was seen and remembered by an old creditor who has thrown him into prison.

SIR GEORGE
I am very glad to hear it.

BLUNTLY
But the young woman, Sir, has been so short a time in town, she has, seemingly, a great deal of modesty and virtue.

SIR GEORGE
And I am very glad to hear of that too—I like her the better—you know I do—for I am weary of that ready compliance I meet with from the sex.

BLUNTLY
But if I might presume to advise, sir—as you are so soon to be married to her ladyship, whom you love with sincere affection, you should give up this pursuit.

SIR GEORGE
And I shall give it up, Bluntly, before my marriage takes place—for, short as that time may be, I expect this passion will be over and forgotten, long before the interval has passed away.—But that brother you were mentioning—

BLUNTLY
I have some reason to think, that with all his poverty, he has a notion of honour.

SIR GEORGE [Laughing]
Oh! I have often tried the effect of a purse of gold with people of honour.—Have you desired them to be sent for as I ordered.

BLUNTLY
I have, Sir.

SIR GEORGE
See if they are come.

[Exit **BLUNTLY**.

Ah! my dear Lady Caroline, it is you, and only you, whom I love with a sincere passion! but in waiting this long expected event of our marriage, permit me to indulge some less exalted wishes.

[Enter **BLUNTLY**.

SIR GEORGE
Are they come?

BLUNTLY

The young man is in the anti-chamber, sir, but his sister is not with him.
[Speaking to **HENRY** who is without]
Please to walk this way—my master desires to see you.

SIR GEORGE
No, no, no—I do not desire to see him, if his sister is not there.—Zounds you scoundrel what did you call him in for?

[Enter **HENRY**, and bows.

[**SIR GEORGE** looks at him with a careless familiarity—**BLUNTLY** leaves the room.

SIR GEORGE
Young man, I am told you are very poor—you may have heard that I am very rich—and I suppose you are acquainted with the extensive meaning of the word—generosity.

HENRY [After an hesitation]
Perhaps not, sir.

SIR GEORGE
The meaning of it, as I comprehend, is, for the rich to give to the poor.—Have you any thing to ask of me in which I can serve you?

HENRY
Your proposal is so general, I am at a loss what to answer—but you are no doubt acquainted with the extensive meaning of the word, pride,—and that will apologize for the seeming indifference with which I receive your offer.

SIR GEORGE
Your pride seems extensive indeed.—I heard your father was in prison, and I pitied him.

HENRY
Did you, Sir?—Did you pity my father:—I beg your pardon—if I have said any thing to offend you pray forgive it—nor let my rudeness turn your companion away from him, to any other object.

SIR GEORGE
Would a small sum release him from confinement? Would about a hundred pounds—

HENRY
I have no doubt but it would.

SIR GEORGE
Then take that note.—Be not surprised—I mean to dispose of a thousand guineas this way, instead of fitting up a theatre in my own house.—That—
[Giving him the note]
—is a mere trifle; my box at the opera, or my dinner; I mean to dine alone to morrow, instead of inviting company.

HENRY

Sir George, I spoke so rudely to you at first, that I know no other way to shew my humility, than to accept your present without reluctance.—I do therefore, as the gift of benevolence, not as the insult of better fortune.

SIR GEORGE

You have a brother, have not you?

HENRY

No, Sir—and only one sister.

SIR GEORGE

A sister is it? well, let me see your father and your brother—your sister I mean—did not you say?—you said a sister, did not you?

HENRY

Yes, Sir.

SIR GEORGE

Well, let me see your father and her; they will rejoice at their good fortune I imagine, and I wish to be a witness of their joy.

HENRY

I will this moment go to our lawyer, extricate my father, and we will all return and make you the spectator of the happiness you have bestowed. Forgive my eagerness to disclose your bounty, sir, if, before I have said half I feel, I fly to reveal it to my father; to whom I can more powerfully express my sensations—than in your presence.

[Exit.

SIR GEORGE

That bait has taken—and now, if the sister will only be as grateful.

[Enter **BLUNTLY**.

BLUNTLY

Dear sir, what can you have said to the young man? I never saw a person so much affected!

SIR GEORGE

In what manner?

BLUNTLY

The tears ran down his cheeks as he passed along, and he held something in his hand which he pressed to his lips, and then to his heart, as if it was a treasure.

SIR GEORGE

It is a treasure, Bluntly—a hundred Guineas.

BLUNTLY

But for which, I believe, you expect a greater treasure in return.

SIR GEORGE

Dost think so Bluntly?—dost think the girl is worth a hundred pounds?

BLUNTLY

If she refuses, she is worth a thousand—but if she complies, you have thrown away your money.

SIR GEORGE

Just the reverse.

BLUNTLY

But I hope, sir, you do not mean to throw away any more thus—for although this sum, by way of charity, may be well applied, yet indeed, sir, I know some of your creditors as much in want as this poor family.

SIR GEORGE

How!—You are in pay by some of my creditors I suppose?

BLUNTLY

No, Sir, you must pay them, before they can pay any body.

SIR GEORGE

You are impertinent—leave the room instantly, and go in search of this sister; now, while the son is gone to release his father.—Tell her, her brother is here, and bring her hither immediately.

BLUNTLY

But, sir, if you will only give me leave to speak one word—

SIR GEORGE

Do, speak;

[Goes to the chimney-piece and takes down a pistol]

—only speak a single syllable, and I'll send a ball instantly through your head.

BLUNTLY

I am dumb, Sir—I don't speak indeed, Sir—upon my life I don't. I wish I may die if I speak a word.

SIR GEORGE

Go on the errand I told you; and if you dare to return without the girl this is your fate.

[Holding up the pistol.

BLUNTLY

Yes, Sir.

[Exit.

SIR GEORGE [Laying the pistol on the table]
Impertinent puppy; to ruffle the temper of a man of fashion with hints of prudence and morality, and paying his debts—all this from a servant too. The insolent, chattering—

[Enter **BLUNTLY**.

BLUNTLY
May I speak now, sir?

SIR GEORGE
What have you to say?

BLUNTLY
Mr. Blackman, sir.

SIR GEORGE
Bid him come in.

[Enter **BLACKMAN**

[Exit **BLUNTLY**.

SIR GEORGE
Good morning, Mr. Blackman; come, sit down.

BLACKMAN [Bowing respectfully]
I am glad, Sir George, I have found you alone, for I come to speak to you on important business.

SIR GEORGE
Business!—no—not now if you please.

BLACKMAN
But I must, sir—I have been here ten times before, and have been put off, but now you must hear what I have to say.

SIR GEORGE
Don't be long then—don't be tedious, Mr. Blackman—for I expect a, a—in short, I expect a pretty woman.

BLACKMAN
When she comes, I will go.

SIR GEORGE
Very well, speak quickly then. What have you to say?

BLACKMAN

I come to speak upon the subject of your father's will; by which you know, you run the hazard of losing great part of what he left behind.

SIR GEORGE
But what am I to do?

BLACKMAN
There is no time to be lost. Consider, that Mr. Manly, the lawyer, whom your father employed, is a man who pretends to a great deal of morality; and it was he who, when your father found himself dying, alarmed his conscience, and persuaded him to make this Will in favour of a second person. Now, I think that you and I both together, ought to have a meeting with this conscientious lawyer.

SIR GEORGE
But I should imagine, Mr. Blackman, that if he is really a conscientious man, you and he will not be upon good terms.

BLACKMAN
Oh! people of our avocation differ in respect to conscience. Puzzle, confound, and abuse each other, and yet are upon good terms.

SIR GEORGE
But I fear—

BLACKMAN
Fear nothing.—There are a vast number of resources in our art.—It is so spacious, and yet so confined—so sublime, and yet so profound—so distinct, and yet so complicated—that if ever this person with whom your fortune is divided should be found, I know how to envelope her in a labyrinth, where she shall be lost again in a hurry.—But your father's lawyer being a very honest—I mean a very particular man in his profession,—I have reason to fear we cannot gain him over to our purpose.—If, therefore,—

[Enter **BLUNTLY**.

SIR GEORGE
My visitor is come, as I told you.

BLACKMAN [Rising]
And I am gone, as I told you.

[Going.

[Enter **ELEANOR**.

BLACKMAN [Aside]
My lodger! ah! ah!
[To her in a whisper]
You may stay another quarter.

[Exit.

SIR GEORGE [To **ELEANOR**]

I am glad to see you.—Bluntly—

[Makes a sign to him to leave the room.

BLUNTLY

Sir?

[**SIR GEORGE** waves his hand and nods his head a second time.

BLUNTLY

Sir?—

[Still affecting not to understand him.

SIR GEORGE [Angrily]

I bid you go.

BLUNTLY

You bid me go, sir?—Oh yes, sir.—Very well, sir.—But indeed, sir, I did not hear you before, sir.—Indeed I did not.

[Bows, and exit with reluctance, which **ELEANOR** observes.

ELEANOR

Pardon me, sir.—I understood my brother was here, but I find he is not.

SIR GEORGE

He is but this instant gone, and will return immediately.—Stay then with me till he comes.

[Takes her hand.

Surely you cannot refuse to remain with me a few moments; especially as I have a great deal to say to you that may tend to your advantage. Why do you cast your eyes with such impatience on that door?

[Goes and locks it.

There, now you may look at it in vain.

ELEANOR

For heaven sake, why am I locked in?

SIR GEORGE

Because you should not escape.

ELEANOR

That makes me resolve I will—Open the door, sir.

[Going to it.

SIR GEORGE
Nay, listen to me. Your sentiments, I make no doubt, are formed from books.

ELEANOR
No, from misfortunes—yet more instructive.

SIR GEORGE
You shall never know misfortune more—you, nor your relations.—But this moment I presented your brother with a sum of money, and he left me with professions of the deepest gratitude.

ELEANOR
My brother!—Has he received money from you? Ah! he promised me he'd not disgrace his family.

SIR GEORGE
How! Family, indeed!

ELEANOR [Raising her voice]
I cannot remain here a moment longer. Open the door, sir—open it immediately.

BLUNTLY [Without]
Sir, sir, sir,—open the door, if you please—you are wanted, sir.

SIR GEORGE
S'death! who can want me in such haste?

[Opens the door, and appears confounded.

[Enter **BLUNTLY**.

SIR GEORGE
Well, sir!

BLUNTLY
—Did you call, sir?

SIR GEORGE
It was you who called, sir.

BLUNTLY
Who, I, sir?

SIR GEORGE
Yes, sir, you—Who wants me?

BLUNTLY [Looking at **ELEANOR**]

Perhaps it was you that called, Ma'am.

ELEANOR
It was I that called: and pray be so kind as to conduct me to my own lodgings.

[**BLUNTLY** offers her his hand.

SIR GEORGE
Dare not to touch her—or to stay another moment in the room.—Begone.

[**BLUNTLY** looks at **ELEANOR** aside, and points to the pistol; then bows humbly, and retires.

SIR GEORGE
And now, my fair Lucretia—

[He is going to seize her—she takes up the pistol and presents it.

ELEANOR
No, it's not myself I'll kill—'Tis you.

SIR GEORGE [Starting]
Nay, nay, nay, lay it down.—Lay that foolish thing down; I beg you will.
[Trembling]
It is charged—it may go off.

ELEANOR
I mean it to go off.

SIR GEORGE
But no jesting—I never liked jesting in my life.

ELEANOR
Nor I—but am always serious.—Dare not, therefore, insult me again, but let me go to my wretched apartments.

[Passes by him, presenting the pistol.

SIR GEORGE
Go to the—

[She turns short at the door, and presents it again.

SIR GEORGE
What would you do?—Here Bluntly! Bluntly!

[Exit **ELEANOR**.

[Enter **BLUNTLY**.

BLUNTLY
Did you call or no, sir?

SIR GEORGE
Yes, sir, I did call now.
[In a threatening accent]
Don't you think you have behaved very well this morning?

BLUNTLY
Yes, sir, I think I have.

SIR GEORGE
I am not joking.

BLUNTLY
Nor am I, sir.

SIR GEORGE
And do not you think I should behave very well, if I was to discharge you my service?

BLUNTLY
As well as can be expected, sir.

SIR GEORGE
Why did you break in upon me just now? Did you think I was going to murder the girl?

BLUNTLY
No, sir, I suspected neither love nor murder.

SIR GEORGE
What then did you suspect?

BLUNTLY
Why, sir, if I may make bold to speak—I was afraid the poor girl might be robbed: and of all she is worth in the world.

SIR GEORGE [Smiling with contempt]
Blockhead! I suppose you mean her virtue?

BLUNTLY
Why, to say the truth, sir, virtue is a currency that grows scarce in the world now-a-days—and some men are so much in need of it, that they think nothing of stopping a harmless female passenger in her road through life, and plundering her of it without remorse, though its loss, embitters every hour she must afterwards pass in her journey.

[Enter **HENRY**.

HENRY

Sir George, my father, liberated from prison by your bounty, is come gratefully to offer—

[Enter **WILLFORD** and **ELEANOR**.

ELEANOR [Holding her **FATHER** by the hand, to prevent his going forward]
Oh, my father! whither are you going? Turn back—turn back.

HENRY [To his **FATHER**]
This is your benefactor—the man whose benevolence has put an end to your sufferings.

[**ELEANOR** bursts into tears and retires up the stage.

WILLFORD

How, sir, can I ever repay what I owe to you?—or how describe those emotions, which your goodness at this moment makes me feel?

SIR GEORGE [In confusion]
Very well—very well—'tis all very well.
[Aside]
I wish it was.—
[To him]
I am glad I have been of service to you.

WILLFORD

You have been like mercy to us all. My daughter's gratitude overflows in tears.—But why, my child, do you keep apart from us? Can you be too timid to confess your obligation?

SIR GEORGE

Let her alone—let her indulge her humour.

WILLFORD

Speak, Eleanor.

SIR GEORGE

No, I had rather she would be silent.

WILLFORD

You offend me by this obstinacy.

ELEANOR [Going to **WILLFORD** and taking his hand]
Oh, my father!—Oh! I cannot—I cannot speak.

WILLFORD

Wherefore?—Explain this moment, what agitates you thus.

ELEANOR

You must return to confinement again.

WILLFORD
How?

ELEANOR
The money that has set you free, was given for the basest purposes—and by a man as far beneath you in principle, as you are beneath him in fortune. Disdain the obligation—and come my father, return to prison.

WILLFORD
Yes.—And with more joy than I left it.
[To **SIR GEORGE**]
Joy, in my daughter's virtuous contempt of thee.
[To his **CHILDREN**]
Leave the house instantly.

[Exit **HENRY** and **ELEANOR**.

WILLFORD [Addressing himself to **SIR GEORGE**]
Your present is but deposited in a lawyer's hands, whose word gained me my liberty—he shall immediately return it to you, while I return to imprisonment.

SIR GEORGE
If the money is in a lawyer's hands, my good friend, it may be some time before you get it returned.

[Going.

WILLFORD
Stay, Sir George—

[He returns.

And look me in the face while you insult me.

[**SIR GEORGE** looks on the floor.

You cannot.—I therefore triumph, while you stand before me abashed like a culprit.—Yet be assured, unthinking, dissipated man, that with all your insolence and cruelty towards me and mine, I have still the charity to rejoice, even for your sake, at seeing you thus confounded. This shame is at least one trait in your favour; and while it revenges my wrongs, gives me joy to find, you are not a hardened libertine.

[Exeunt.

ACT III

SCENE I - The Apartment at Sir George Splendorville's

The night has been passed at play—Several card-tables with company playing—**SIR GEORGE** and **LADY CAROLINE** at the same table. **SIR GEORGE** rises furiously.

SIR GEORGE
Never was the whole train of misfortunes so united to undo a man, as this night to ruin me. The most obstinate round of ill luck—

MR. LUCRE [Waking from a sleep]
What is all that? You have lost a great deal of money, I suppose?

SIR GEORGE
Every guinea I had about me, and fifteen thousand besides, for which I have given my word.

MR. LUCRE
Fifteen thousand guineas! and I have not won one of them.—Oh, confusion upon every thing that has prevented me.

SIR GEORGE [Taking **LADY CAROLINE** aside]
Lady Caroline, you are the sole person who has profited by my loss.—Prove to me that your design was not to ruin me; to sink me into the abyss of misfortune,—prove to me, you love me in return for all my tender love to you. And—
[Taking up the cards]
—give me my revenge in one single cut.

LADY CAROLINE
If this is the proof you require, I consent.

SIR GEORGE
Thank you.—And it is for double or quit.—Thank you.

[She shuffles and cuts.

SIR GEORGE
Ay, it will be mine—thank you.—I shall be the winner—thank you.

[He cuts—then tears the cards and throws them on the floor.

Destraction!—Furies of the blackest kind conspire against me, and all their serpents are in my heart.—Cruel, yet beloved woman! Could you thus abuse and take advantage of the madness of my situation?

LADY CAROLINE
Your misfortunes, my dear Sir George—make you blind.

SIR GEORGE [Taking her again aside]
No, they have rather opened my eyes, and have shown me what you are.—Still an object I adore; but I now perceive your are one to my ruin devoted.—If any other intention had directed you, would you have thus decoyed me to my folly?—You know my proneness to play, your own likelihood of success,

and have palpably allured me to my destruction. Ungrateful woman, you never loved me, but taught me to believe so, in order to partake of my prodigality.—Do not be suspicious, madam; the debt shall be discharged within a week.

LADY CAROLINE [With the utmost indifference]
That will do, sir—I depend upon your word; and that will do.

[Exit curtsying.

SIR GEORGE
Ungrateful—cruel—she is gone without giving me one hope.—She even insults—despises me.

MR. LUCRE [Coming forward]
Indeed, my dear friend, I compassionate your ill luck most feelingly; and yet I am nearly as great an object of compassion on this occasion as yourself; for I have not won a single guinea of all your losses: if I had, why I could have borne your misfortune with some sort of patience.

LADY BRIDGET
My dear Sir George, your situation affects me so extremely, I cannot stay a moment longer in your presence.

[Goes to the door, and returns.

But you may depend upon my prayers.

[Exit.

LORD HAZARD
Sir George, if I had any consolation to offer, it should be at your service—but you know—you are convinced—I have merely a sufficiency of consolation—that is, of friends and of money to support myself in the rank of life I hold in the world. For without that—without that rank—I sincerely wish you a good morning.

[Exit **LORD HAZARD**.

SIR GEORGE
Good morning.

[The **COMPANY** by degrees all steal out of the room, except **MR LUCRE**.

SIR GEORGE [Looking around]
Where are all my guests?—the greatest part gone without a word in condolence, and the rest torturing me with insulting wishes. Here! behold! here is the sole reliance which I have prepared for the hour of misfortune; and what is it?—words—compliments—desertion—and from those, whose ingratitude makes their neglect still more poignant.

[Turns and perceives **MR LUCRE**.

Lucre, my dear Lucre, are not you amazed at what you see?

MR. LUCRE
No, not at all—'tis the way of the world—we caress our acquaintances whilst they are happy and in power, but if they fall into misfortune, we think we do enough if we have the good nature to pity them.

SIR GEORGE
And are you, one of these friends?

MR. LUCRE
I am like the rest of the world.—I was in the number of your flatterers; but at present you have none—for you may already perceive, we are grown sincere.

SIR GEORGE
But have not you a thousand times desired me, in any distress, to prove you?

MR. LUCRE
And you do prove me now, do you not?—Heaven bless you.

[Shaking hands with him.

I shall always have a regard for you—but for any thing farther—I scorn professions which I do not mean to keep.

[Going.

SIR GEORGE
Nay, but Lucre! consider the anguish in which you leave me!—consider, that to be forsaken by my friends is more affecting than the loss of all my fortune. Though you have nothing else to give me, yet give me your company.

MR. LUCRE
My dear friend I cannot. Reflect that I am under obligations to you—so many indeed that I am ashamed to see you.—I am naturally bashful; and do not be surprised if I should never have the confidence to look you in the face again.

[Exit.

SIR GEORGE
This is the world, such as I have heard it described, but not such as I could ever believe it to be.—But I forgive—I forget all the world except Lady Caroline—her ingratitude fastens to my heart and drives me to despair. She, on whom I have squandered so much—she, whom I loved—and whom I still love, spite of her perfidy!

[Enter **BLUNTLY**.

Well, Bluntly—behold the friendship of the friends I loved! This morning I was in prosperity and had many—this night I am ruined, and I have not one.

BLUNTLY
Ruined, sir?

SIR GEORGE
Totally: and shall be forced to part with every thing I possess to pay the sums I owe.—Of course, I shall part with all my servants—and do you endeavour to find some other place.

BLUNTLY
But first, sir,—permit me to ask a favour of you?

SIR GEORGE
A favour of me? I have no favours now to grant.

BLUNTLY
I beg your pardon, sir—you have one—and I entreat it on my knees.

SIR GEORGE
What would you ask of me?

BLUNTLY
To remain along with you still.—I will never quit you; but serve you for nothing, to the last moment of my life.

SIR GEORGE
I have then one friend left.

[Embracing him.

And never will I forget to acknowledge the obligation.

[Enter **BLACKMAN**.

BLACKMAN
Pardon me—sir—I beg ten thousand pardons—pray excuse me, [In the most servile manner] for entering before I sent to know if you were at leisure—but your attendants are all fast asleep on the chairs of your antichamber.—I could not wake a soul—and I imagined you yourself were not yet up.

SIR GEORGE
On the contrary, I have not yet been in bed. And when I do go there, I wish never to rise from it again.

BLACKMAN
Has any thing unexpected happened?

SIR GEORGE
Yes.—That I am ruined—inevitably ruined—Behold—

[Shewing the cards.

—the only wreck of my fortune.

BLACKMAN [Starting]
Lost all your fortune?

SIR GEORGE
All I am worth—and as much more as I am worth.

[**BLACKMAN** draws a chair, sits down with great familiarity, and stares **SIR GEORGE** rudely in the face.

BLACKMAN
Lost all you are worth? He, he, he, he!
[Laughs maliciously]
Pretty news, truly! Why then I suppose I have lost great part of what I am worth? all which you are indebted to me?—However there is a way yet to retrieve you. But—please to desire your servant to leave the room.

SIR GEORGE
Bluntly, leave us a moment.

[Exit **BLUNTLY**]

Well, Mr. Blackman, what is this grand secret?

BLACKMAN
Why, in the state to which you have reduced yourself, there is certainly no one hope for you, but in that portion, that half of your fortune, which the will of your father keeps you out of.

SIR GEORGE
But how am I to obtain it? The lawyer in whose hands it is placed, will not give it up, without being insured from any future demand by some certain proofs.

BLACKMAN
And suppose I should search, and find proofs? Suppose I have them already by me?—But upon this occasion, you must not only rely implicitly on what I say, but it is necessary you should say the same yourself.

SIR GEORGE
If you advance no falsehood, I cannot have any objection.

BLACKMAN
Falsehood!—falsehood!—I apprehend, Sir George, you do not consider, that there is a particular construction put upon words and phrases in the practice of the law, which the rest of the world, out of that study, are not clearly acquainted with. For instance, falsehood with us, is not exactly what it is with other people.

SIR GEORGE

How! Is truth, immutable truth, to be corrupted and confounded by men of the law?

BLACKMAN

I was not speaking of truth—that, we have nothing to do with.

SIR GEORGE

I, must not say so, however, sir.—And in this crisis of my sufferings, it is the only comfort, the only consolatory reflection left me, that truth and I, will never separate.

BLACKMAN

Stick to your truth—but confide in me as usual.—You will go with me, then, to Mr. Manly, your father's lawyer, and corroborate all that I shall say?

SIR GEORGE

Tell me, but what you intend to say?

BLACKMAN

I can't do that. In the practice of the law, we never know what we intend to say—and therefore our blunders, when we make them, are in some measure excusable—and if I should chance to make a blunder or two, I mean any trivial mistake, when we come before this lawyer, you must promise not to interfere, or in any shape contradict me.

SIR GEORGE

A mere lapse of memory, I have nothing to do with.

BLACKMAN

And my memory grows very bad; therefore you must not disconcert me.

SIR GEORGE

Come, let us begone—I am ready to go with you this moment.

BLACKMAN

I must first go home, and prepare a few writings.

SIR GEORGE

But call to mind that I rely upon your honour.

BLACKMAN

Do you think Bluntly, your servant, is an honest man?

SIR GEORGE

I am sure he is.

BLACKMAN

Then, to quiet your fears, I will take him along with us; and you will depend on what he shall say, I make no doubt?

SIR GEORGE

I would stake my being upon his veracity.

BLACKMAN
Call him in, then, and bid him do as I command him.

SIR GEORGE
Here, Bluntly.

[Enter **BLUNTLY**.

Mr. Blackman has some business with you—listen to him with attention, and follow his directions.

[Exit.

BLACKMAN
You know, I suppose, the perilous situation of your master?

[**BLUNTLY** shakes his head, and wipes his eyes.

BLACKMAN
Good fellow! good fellow!—and you would, I dare say, do any thing to rescue him from the misery with which he is surrounded?

BLUNTLY
I would lay down my life.

BLACKMAN
You can do it for less. Only put on a black coat, and the business is done.

BLUNTLY
What's that all? Oh! if I can save him by putting on a black coat, I'll go buy mourning, and wear it all my life.

BLACKMAN
There's a good fellow. I sincerely thank you for this attachment to your master.

[Shaking him by the hand.

BLUNTLY
My dear Blackman, I beg your pardon for what I am going to say; but as you behave thus friendly on this unfortunate occasion, I must confess to you—that till now I always hated you.—I could not bear the sight of you.—For I thought you (I wish I may die if I did not) one of the greatest rogues in the world. I fancied you only waited on, and advised my master to make your market of him.—But now your attention to him in his distress, when all his friends have forsaken him, is so kind—Heaven bless you— Heaven bless you—I'll go buy a black coat.

[Going.

BLACKMAN

I have something more to say to you.—When you have put on this coat, you must meet your master and me at Mr. Manly's, the lawyer; and when we are all there, you must mind and say, exactly what I say.

BLUNTLY

And what will that be?

BLACKMAN

Oh! something.

BLUNTLY

I have no objection to say something—but I hope you won't make me say any thing.

BLACKMAN

You seem to doubt me once more, sir?

BLUNTLY

No, I am doubting you now for the first time; for I always thought I was certain before.

BLACKMAN

And will you not venture to say yes, and no, to what I shall advance?

BLUNTLY

Why—I think I may venture to say yes to your no, and no to your yes, with a safe conscience.

BLACKMAN

If you do not instantly follow me and do all that I shall propose, your master is ruined.—Would you see him dragged to prison?

BLUNTLY

No, I would sooner go myself.

BLACKMAN

Then why do you stand talking about a safe conscience. Half my clients would have been ruined if I had shewn my zeal as you do. Conscience indeed! Why, this is a matter of law, to serve your master in his necessity.

BLUNTLY

I have heard necessity has no law—but if it has no conscience, it is a much worse thing than I took it for.—No matter for that—come along.—Oh my poor master!—I would even tell a lie to save him.

[Exeunt.

SCENE II - A Lawyer's Study

MR. MANLY discovered at his writing-desk—a **SERVANT** attending.

MANLY
Who do you say wants to speak with me?

SERVANT
Mr. Lucre, sir.

MANLY
And who else?

SERVANT
A person who says his name is Willford, he looks as if he came from the country, and seems in mean circumstances.

MANLY
Show him to me directly. And take Mr. Lucre, or any other person of fashion that may call, to my clerks.

[Exit **SERVANT**.

But for the poor, let them be under my protection.

[Enter **WILLFORD** and **ELEANOR**.

MANLY
Come in—walk in, and let me know what I can do to serve you.

WILLFORD
I deposited, sir, in your clerk's hands, a sum of money to set me free from confinement for debt.—On his word, I was discharged—he owns he has not yet paid away this money, still he refuses to restore it to me, though in return I again render up my person.

MANLY
And why would you do this?

WILLFORD
Because my honour—I mean my conscience—for that's the poor man's honour—is concerned.

MANLY
Explain yourself.

WILLFORD
A son of mine, received this sum I speak of, and thought it given him; while it was only meant as a purchase—a purchase of what we had no right to sell—and therefore it must be restored to the owner.

MANLY
And who is he?

WILLFORD

Sir George Splendorville—I suppose you have heard of him?

MANLY
He, you mean, who by the desire of his father's will, lately changed his name from Blandford?

WILLFORD
Sir!

MANLY
The name, which some part of the family, while reduced, had taken.

WILLFORD
Good Heaven! Is there such a circumstance in his story?

MANLY
Why do you ask with such emotion?

WILLFORD
Because he is the man, in search of whom I left my habitation in the country, to present before him a destitute young woman, a near relation.

MANLY
What relation?—Be particular in your answer.

WILLFORD
A sister.

MANLY
I thank you for your intelligence. You have named a person who for these three years past, I have in vain endeavoured to find.—But did you say she was in poverty?

WILLFORD
I did.

MANLY
I give you joy then—for I have in my possession a deed which conveys to a lost daughter of Sir George's father, the other half of the fortune he bequeathed his son—but as yet, all my endeavours have been in vain to find where she, and an uncle, to whose care she was entrusted in her infancy, are retired.

WILLFORD [Turning to **ELEANOR**]
Now, Eleanor, arm yourself with fortitude—with fortitude to bear not the frowns, but the smiles of fortune. Be humble, collected, and the same you have ever been, while I for the first time inform you— you are not my daughter.—And from this gentleman's intelligence add, you are rich—you are the deceased Blandford's child, and Splendorville's sister.

ELEANOR
Oh! Heavens! Do I lose a father such as you, to gain a brother such as he is?

MANLY [To **WILLFORD**]

There can be no mistake on this occasion—And you, if I am not deceived, are the brother of the late Mr. Blandford. Your looks, your person, your very voice confirms it.

WILLFORD

I have writings in my care, shall prove it beyond a doubt; with the whole narrative of our separation when he with his son, then a youth, embarked for India; where I suppose, riches, soon succeeded poverty.

[Enter **SERVANT**.

SERVANT

Lady Caroline Seymour, sir, is at the door in her carriage, and will not be denied admittance. She says she must see you upon some very urgent business.

MANLY [To **WILLFORD** and **ELEANOR**]

Will you do me the favour to step for a moment into this room? Lady Caroline will not stay long. I'll not detain you.

[Exit **WILLFORD** and **ELEANOR**.

[Enter **LADY CAROLINE**.

LADY CAROLINE

Dear Mr. Manly, I have a thousand apologies to make—And yet I am sure you will excuse the subject of my visit, when you consider—

MANLY

Your ladyship will please to sit down.

[He draws chairs and they sit.

LADY CAROLINE

You cannot be ignorant, Mr. Manly—you must know, the terms of acquaintance on which Sir George Splendorville and I have been, for some time past?—you were his father's agent; his chief solicitor; and although you are not employed by Sir George, yet the state of his affairs cannot be concealed from you—Has he, or has he not, any inheritance yet to come?

MANLY

Pardon me, madam—though not entrusted by Sir George, I will, nevertheless, keep his secrets.

LADY CAROLINE

That is plainly telling me he is worth nothing.

MANLY

By no means—Sir George, in spite of his profusion, must still be rich. He has preserved his large estate in Wales; and as to money, I do not doubt but he has a considerable sum.

LADY CAROLINE
Not a guinea. I won it all from him last night.

MANLY
You? You, who are to become his wife?

LADY CAROLINE
I might, had I not been thus fortunate. But why should I marry him, when his riches are mine, without that ceremony.

MANLY
Inconsiderate man!—what will be the end of his imprudence! Yet, Heaven be praised! he has still that fine estate, I just now mentioned.

LADY CAROLINE
Indeed he has not—that has belonged to me these three months.

MANLY
To you!

LADY CAROLINE
Yes—Bought for me under another name by agents; and for half its value.

MANLY
Madman!—Yet your ladyship must excuse me. I know your income stinted, and till the death of the Earl, your father, where could you raise sufficient to make even half the purchase.

LADY CAROLINE
From Splendorville's own prodigality—from lavish presents made to me by him.

[Enter **SERVANT**.

SERVANT
Sir George Splendorville, sir, desires to speak with you—he is at the door with Mr. Blackman.

LADY CAROLINE
Oh Heavens! do not let him see me here.

[She is hastening to the room where **WILLFORD** and his **DAUGHTER** are.

MANLY
I have company there—walk in here, if you Please.

[Shows her another door and she enters.

MANLY [To the **SERVANT**]
Desire Sir George to walk in.

[Enter **SIR GEORGE** and **BLACKMAN**.

MANLY
Sir George, do me the favour to sit down.

[He looks coolly on **BLACKMAN**, and pointing to a chair says Good morning. They sit.

SIR GEORGE
Mr. Manly, my attorney will let you know the business on which I am come.

BLACKMAN
Why yes, Mr. Manly, it is extremely hard that Sir George has for so long a time been kept out of a very large part of his fortune; particularly, as he has had occasion for it.

SIR GEORGE
I have had occasion for it I assure you Mr. Manly; and I have occasion for it at this very time.

MR. MANLY
But so may the person, sir, from whom you would take it. In a word, Sir George, neither your lawyer nor you, shall prevail on me to give up the trust reposed in me by your father, without certain evidence, that your sister will never come to make her claim.

BLACKMAN
You are not afraid of ghosts, are you?

MANLY
No, nor of robbers either:—you cannot frighten me, Mr. Blackman.

BLACKMAN
Then depend upon it, the sister of Sir George can never appear in any other manner than as a spirit. For, here, sir,—

[Taking from his pocket a parcel of papers.

—here are authentic letters to prove her death.

[**SIR GEORGE** looks confused.

MANLY
Her death!

BLACKMAN
Yes, her death. Here is a certificate from the curate of the parish in which she was buried.

MANLY
Buried too!

BLACKMAN

Yes, sir, buried. Here is also an affidavit from the sexton of the said village, signed by the overseer and churchwardens, testifying the same.—You see,

[Shewing him the paper, and reading at the fame time.

"Died Anno Domini, one thousand seven hundred and eighty nine, the seventeenth of June—"

[MR MANLY takes the paper, and while he is reading, SIR GEORGE says apart—

SIR GEORGE
How near to the brink of infamy has my imprudence led me! And s'death, my confusion takes from me the power to explain, and expose the scoundrel.
Mr. Manly, I will leave you for the present; but you shall hear from me shortly,—when this matter shall be accounted for clearly—perfectly to your satisfaction, you may depend upon it.—

[Going.

MANLY
Stay, Sir George, and—

BLACKMAN
Aye, Sir George, stay and see Mr. Manly's objections wholly removed. He seems to doubt the evidence of paper; I must, therefore, beg leave to produce a living witness—the gentleman whom I appointed to meet me here.

MANLY
And who is he?

BLACKMAN
The apothecary, who attended Sir George's sister in her dying illness.

[SIR GEORGE starts.

MANLY
Desire him to walk in by all means. What is the matter, Sir George, you look discomposed?

BLACKMAN
Sir George is something nervous, Mr. Manly; and you know the very name of a medical gentleman, will affect the nerves of some people.

[BLACKMAN goes to the door, and leads on BLUNTLY, dressed in mourning.

SIR GEORGE [Aside]
Bluntly!—But I will see the end of this.

MANLY [Bowing to him]
You are an apothecary, I think, sir?

[**BLUNTLY** looks at **BLACKMAN**.

BLACKMAN
Yes, sir.

BLUNTLY [After seeming inclined to say, No]
Yes, sir.

MANLY
Pray sir, what disorder took the young lady, on whose account you have been brought hither, out of the world?

[**BLUNTLY** looks at **BLACKMAN**.

BLACKMAN
Oh! the old disorder, I suppose.

BLUNTLY
The old disorder.

MANLY
And pray what may that be, sir?

[**BLACKMAN** offers to reply.

Mr. Blackman, Please to let this gentleman speak for himself.—What is it you mean, pray sir, by the old disorder?

BLUNTLY
I—I—mean—Love, sir.

MANLY
You will not pretend to say, that love, was the cause of her death?

BLUNTLY [Confused and hesitating]
That—and a few fits of the gout.

MANLY
I fear, sir, you are not in perfect health yourself—you tremble and look very pale.

BLACKMAN
That is because the subject affects him.

MANLY
Do you then never mention the young lady without being affected?

BLUNTLY

Never, sir—for had you seen her as I did—um—Had you seen her.—She was in very great danger from the first; but after I attended her, she was in greater danger still.—I advised a physician to be called in; on which she grew worse.—We had next a consultation of physicians; and then it was all over with her.

SIR GEORGE [Rising from his chair]
Blackman, this is too much—all my calamities are inferior to this—Desist, therefore, or—

BLACKMAN [To **BLUNTLY**]
Desist—He cannot bear to hear the pathetic description. Consider the lady was his sister—and though he had not the pleasure of knowing her—yet, poor thing—
[Affecting to weep]
—poor young woman! he cannot help lamenting her loss.

BLUNTLY [Pretending to weep also]
No more can I—for though she was not my relation—yet she was my Patient.

SIR GEORGE
I can bear no more.—Mr. Manly, you are imposed upon. But think not, however appearances may be against me, that I came here as the tool of so infamous a deceit.—Thoughtlessness, Mr. Manly, has embarrassed my circumstances; and thoughtlessness alone, has made me employ a villain to retrieve them.

BLACKMAN
Mighty fine!

SIR GEORGE
I have no authority, sir, to affirm, that my sister is not alive; and I am confident the account you have just now heard, of her death, is but an artifice. My indiscretions have reduced me nearly to beggary; but I will perish in confinement—cheerfully perish—rather than owe my affluence to one dishonourable action.

BLACKMAN
Grief has turned his brain.

MANLY
Sir George, I honour your feelings; and as for the feelings of these gentlemen, I am extremely happy, that it is in my power to dry up their tears, and calm all their sorrows.

SIR GEORGE
Sir!

BLACKMAN
How? In what way?

MANLY [Going to the door where **WILLFORD** and his **NIECE** are]
Come forth, young lady, to the arms of a brother, and relieve the anguish of these mourners, who are lamenting your decease.

[**ELEANOR** and **WILLFORD** enter.

—Yes, Sir George, here is that sister, whom those gentlemen assure us, is dead;—and this is the brother of your father.—These are proofs, as convincing, I hope, as any Mr. Blackman can produce.

SIR GEORGE
She, my sister! Her pretended father my uncle too!
[Aside]
Blackman, you would have plunged me into an anguish I never knew before; you would have plunged me into shame.

BLUNTLY
And so you have me.

BLACKMAN
Pshaw.—Mr. Manly, notwithstanding you are these people's voucher, this appears but a scheme.—These persons are but adventurers, and may possibly have about them forgeries, such as an honest man, like myself, would shudder at.

MANLY
Going to the door. Who's there?

[Enter **SERVANT**.

Shew that—that Mr. Blackman, out of my house instantly; and take care you never admit him again.

BLACKMAN
Sir George, will you suffer this?

SIR GEORGE
Aye, and a great deal more.

BLUNTLY
Look'ee Blackman.—If you don't fall down upon your knees, and beg my pardon at the street door, for the trick you have put upon me, in assuring me my master's sister was really dead, and that I could do her no injury, by doing him a service—if you don't beg my pardon for this, I'll give you such an assault and battery as you never had to do with in your life.

BLACKMAN
Beat me—do, beat me—I'll thank you for beating me—I'd be beat every hour of the day, to recover damages.

[Exit with **BLUNTLY**.

SIR GEORGE
My sister—with the sincerest joy I call you by that name—and while I thus embrace you, offer you a heart, that beats with all the pure and tender affection, which our kindred to each other claims.—In you—

[Embracing his uncle.

I behold my father; and experience an awful fear, mingled with my regard.

WILLFORD
Continue still that regard, and even that fear—these filial sentiments may prove important; and they shall ever be repaid with my paternal watchings, friendship, and love.

ELEANOR
My brother—

SIR GEORGE
I have been unworthy of you—I will be so no more, but imitate your excellence. Yet, when I reflect—

[**LADY CAROLINE** comes softly from the inner apartment, and attends to the discourse.

ELEANOR
My brother, do not imagine—

SIR GEORGE
Leave me, leave me to all the agonies of my misconduct.—Where is my fortune? Now all irrecoverably gone—My last, my only resource is now to be paid to another—I have lost every thing.

LADY CAROLINE
Coming forward. No, Sir George, nothing—since I possess all that was yours.

SIR GEORGE
How!

LADY CAROLINE
Behold a friend in your necessities—a mistress whom your misfortunes cannot drive away—but who, experiencing much of your unkindness, still loves you; and knowing your every folly, will still submit to honour, and obey you.

I received your lavish presents, but to hoard them for you—made myself mistress of your fortune, but to return it to you—and with it, all my own.

SIR GEORGE
Can this be real? Can I be raised in one moment, from the depths of misery to unbounded happiness?

[Enter **SERVANT**.

SERVANT
A young man, who says he is Mr. Willford's son, is called to enquire for him.

MANLY
Shew him in.

[**SIR GEORGE** and **LADY CAROLINE** retire to the back part of the stage.

[Enter **HENRY**.

WILLFORD
Come, Henry, and take leave of your sister for ever.

HENRY
How so, sir?—What do you mean? To be parted from her, would be the utmost rigour of fortune.

MANLY
The affection with which you speak, young gentleman, seems to convey something beyond mere brotherly love.

WILLFORD
I some years since revealed to him she was not his sister.

ELEANOR
And he, some years since, implied it to me. Yet, in such doubtful terms, I knew not which of us had the sorrow not to be your child.—I now find it is myself—and I aver it to be a sorrow, for which, all the fortune I am going to possess will not repay me.

SIR GEORGE
Then, my dearest sister, indulge the hope you may yet be his daughter. This young man's merit deserves a reward, and in time he may learn to love you by a still nearer tie than that, you have so long known to exist between you; nay, even by a nearer tie than that of brother.

HENRY
I am in doubt of what I hear—Eleanor, since our short separation, there cannot surely have been any important discovery—

MANLY
Be not surprised—great discoveries, which we labour in vain for years to make, are frequently brought about in one lucky moment, without any labour at all.

SIR GEORGE
True—for till this day arose, I had passed every hour since my birth, without making one discovery to my advantage—while this short, but propitious morning, has discovered to me all my former folly—and discovered to me—how to be in future happy.

Mrs Inchbald – A Short Biography

Elizabeth Simpson was born on 15th October 1753 at Stanningfield, near Bury St Edmunds, Suffolk. She was the eighth of nine children to John Simpson, a farmer, and his wife, Mary, née Rushbrook. The family were Roman Catholics.

Her brother was educated at school, but Elizabeth, like her sisters, was educated at home. Elizabeth also suffered from a speech impediment, a stammer.

Elizabeth's father had died when she was only eight, leaving her mother to take care of a large family. These were difficult times.

Despite the fact that she suffered from a debilitating stammer she was determined, from a very young age, to become an actress. She had loved theatre from her very first childhood visit.

As a young woman Elizabeth was tall and slender. But this beauty brought with it the many attentions of men. It was double-edged.

Elizabeth had written to the manager of the Norwich Theatre to obtain acting work. He had replied that he would welcome a visit for her to audition. For her young naïve years this seemed like a golden opportunity. However, in 1770 her family forbade her attempt to take on an acting assignment there. They had no such qualms with her brother George, who entered the acting profession.

In April 1772, Elizabeth left, without permission, for London to pursue her chosen career. Although she was successful in obtaining parts her audiences found it difficult to admire her talents given her speech impediment. However, Elizabeth was diligent and hard-working on attempting to overcome this hurdle. She spent much time concentrating on pronunciation in order to eliminate the stammer. She was known to write out the parts she wanted to perform and practice the lines to point of such familiarity that her impediment was banished. Her acting, although at times stilted, especially in monologues, gained praise for her approach, and for her well-developed characters. For the audience she came across as a real person, not just an actor performing a piece. Elizabeth would keenly study the performances of others before she herself performed.

In these early months Elizabeth was young and alone, and reportedly also suffered from the attentions of sexual predators.

In June, merely two months after arriving she accepted an offer of marriage from Joseph Inchbald, a fellow Catholic and actor. They had met before on her previous trips to London, usually to see her brother, George, acting on stage. He had written her several letters proposing marriage which she had declined. But now it seemed the most expedient way to make progress in her career.

By all accounts it was still an odd choice. Joseph was a so-so actor, and at least twice her age as well as being the father of two illegitimate sons. The marriage was to produce no children and was not the happiest of unions.

On 4th September of that year, 1772, Elizabeth and Joseph appeared for the first time together on stage in 'King Lear'. The following month they toured Scotland with the West Digges's theatre company. This was to continue for the next four years.

In 1776 they decided on a change of career and a change of country. They moved to France. Joseph would now learn to paint, and Elizabeth would study French. It was a short-lived disaster. Within a month all their funds were gone and a return to England was necessitated.

They moved to Liverpool, Canterbury and Yorkshire and acted for both the Joseph Younger's company and Tate Wilkinson's company in search of permanency and a recovery from their ill-fortune.

Completely unexpectedly Joseph died in June 1779. Despite her loss Elizabeth continued to perform across the country from Dublin to London and places in between.

In 1780, she joined the Covent Garden Company and played Bellarion in 'Philaster'.

In all Elizabeth's acting career was only moderately successful and lasted some 17 years. However, she appeared in many classical roles as well as new plays such as Hannah Cowley's 'The Belle's Stratagem'. Around the theatre she was known for upholding high moral standards. She later described having to fend off sexual advances from, among others, stage manager James Dodd and theatre manager John Taylor.

It was now in the years after her husband's death that that Elizabeth decided on a new literary path. With no attachments, and acting taking up only some of her time, she decided to write plays.

Her first play to be performed was 'A Mogul Tale or, The Descent of the Balloon', in 1784, in which she also played the leading female role of Selina. The play was premiered at the Haymarket Theatre.

'Lovers' Vows', in 1798, was based on her translation of August von Kotzebues original work and garnered both praise and complements from Jane Austen and was featured as a focus of moral controversy in her novel Mansfield Park. Although Austen's book brought more fame to Elizabeth, 'Lovers' Vows' initially ran for only forty-two nights when originally performed in 1798.

One of the things that separated Elizabeth from other contemporary playwrights was her ability to translate plays from German and French into English and to use them as a foundation. These translations were popular with the public and her talents in bringing the characters to life was instrumental in achieving this.

Her success as a playwright enabled Elizabeth to support herself and not need a new husband to carry out this role. Between 1784 and 1805 she had 19 of her comedies, sentimental dramas, and farces (many of them translations from the French) performed at London theatres, although it is thought she actually wrote between 21 and 23 in total depending on which account you think is most accurate. She is usually credited as Mrs Inchbald.

As well she wrote two novels; 'A Simple Story' was published in 1791 and once referred to as "the most elegant English fiction of the eighteenth century". 'Nature and Art' was published in 1796. Both have been constantly reprinted.

Her four-volume autobiography was destroyed before her death upon the advice of her confessor, but she left a few of her diaries.

In her later years she found time to do a considerable amount of editorial and critical work. In 1805, she decided to try being a theatre critic. This literary excursion, after the praise for her acting and more so for her writing, seemed to be a low point in her achievements. The reception to her work amongst her peer critics was low, one commented upon her ignorance of Shakespeare.

Her career from actress, to playwright and novelist was achieved in difficult times for women to accomplish such things. Indeed, whilst the theatre and its boundaries were quite strict she managed, in her novels, to explore political radicalism. Her good looks together with her passionate and fiery nature attracted a string of admirers but she never re-married. Despite her love of independence, she still desired and sought social respectability.

Mrs Elizabeth Inchbald died on 1st August 1821 in Kensington, London.

She is buried in the churchyard of St Mary Abbots. On her gravestone is written, "Whose writings will be cherished while truth, simplicity, and feelings, command public admiration."

Mrs Inchbald – A Concise Bibliography

Plays

Mogul Tale; or, The Descent of the Balloon (1784)
Appearance is against Them (1785)
I'll Tell you What (1785)
The Widow's Vow (1786)
The Midnight Hour (1787)
Such Things Are (1787)
All on a Summer's Day (1787)
Animal Magnetism (c1788)
The Child of Nature (1788)
The Married Man (1789)
Next Door Neighbours (1791)
Everyone has his Fault (1793)
To Marry, or not to Marry (1793)
The Wedding Day (1794)
Wives as They Were and Maids as They Are (1797)
Lovers' Vows (1798)
The Wise Man of the East (1799)
The Massacre (1792 (not performed)
A Case of Conscience (published 1833)
The Ancient Law (not performed)
The Hue and Cry (unpublished)
Young Men and Old Women (Lovers No Conjurers) (adaptation of Le Méchant; unpublished)

Novels

A Simple Story (1791)
Nature and Art (1796)

www.ingramcontent.com/pod-product-compliance
Lightning Source LLC
Chambersburg PA
CBHW021943040426

42448CB00008B/1220